Fields of Light

A Metaphysical Treatise in Prose Poetry

John Lambert

The author at age 30

Portrait illustrated by Aron Laiken/The Creativity Zone
Containing selections from the 'Instauratio Magnus Opus' 1974-1994

"Here I stand, look all around me
in my paradise
Step into this world
Colors surround me
You should have seen. Oh! Ecstasy
clearly reflects the changing dawn
of a time that used to be"

www.FieldsOfLight.com

Print ISBN: 978-1-09833-575-5
eBook ISBN: 978-1-09833-576-2

Printed in the United States of America

First Edition

PREFACE

The journey of writing these songs and poems began with a near-death experience I had nearly five decades ago. I imagined it would be impossible to express illumination, at-one-ness with the Light, but most pieces contained in this book came through me, effortlessly. My only struggle was to catch them on paper as they ran through my mind, then vanished. Others came when I sat down at the piano and composed.

This enlightenment experience is not unique; it is universal. It is the thread that runs through all systems of Truth. This work is an invitation to explore – no matter our different backgrounds and beliefs – what we are, what is possible, and how to manifest what is humanity at the highest level.

Upon reflection, I believe this work will unpack itself.

ACKNOWLEDGEMENTS

This book of prose-poems and song has been over four decades in the making. It wouldn't have happened without the friends who believed in me and helped me along the way. I thank you - every one of you. It wouldn't have happened without your love and support.

CONTENTS

OVERTURE

We are the giants in the earth
We are the gods of our universe

Every blade of grass, the infinity in a
Moment - And the reasons are for love, and the
equanimity of space, the content of which we are afforded
the necessity of giving light to a wealth of understanding beyond
this quantum leap – for the denouement of life unfolds before our eyes,
we see the infinity of man and the consciousness of love,
the soul song, the energy of life itself.
It tells a tale of lightening up the
skies of our minds, loosens the burden of fear
with the knowledge of life eternal.
We are the giants in the earth.

The distinction in seeking after truth
is in the blueprint of the ages,
and seen but once, and go forever with you, so be it.

Then nourish like a seed the growth of
mind, body, and spirit [is the guiding light, and
a light it is] the spark which lives in the body proper - whose
initial awakening is tantamount to ecstasy nonpareil - that is indeed but
a spark, for it is only the beginning, as compared to
the fruition of which it signals the awakening of a giant in the earth.
As the mind seeks to acquaint itself with the
Inherent design of the body electric,
Dimensia is lost.
Minding the Body awakens the Spirit in man,
avers that this transformation is at hand, figuratively,
and so on and on, until these things are done, we'll
be separate and not one. But by one way, there is, truth.

Love is the energy of the universe.

In it lies our strength to live and to love - again and again - physically,

where this process takes form; mentally, where the decision

and direction to do so were given; wherein the Spirit, substance of all –

Awakened first by the spirit in man, then the body, mind, and back again,

sufficiently energized, achieves equanimity with its parts, and the body entire.

These three agents (body, mind and spirit), then acting as one,

move to become united with that part of life which is spirit - pure energy,

where-there-is-life eternal in spirit - and this is the truth of it:

One by one we will surely come to realize these things.

Some fine time this equanimity we speak of will be reached in ourselves,

and finally, all potential resolved - in the universe as well.

Another cycle will be complete, things will be as they once were, and I can

see it now: Albert's Einstein will read differently than this E=mc2 that we

are presently limited to, and the Pineal equation will read E=E.

So the neophytes will wonder at this, let their minds seek to probe as I have

for the answer that cannot be found [by intellect alone]. So I do this, and here it is:

We are the giants in the earth

We are the gods of our universe

Almighty father in Heaven, thanks be these praises fixed to shine - and it is

the line and rhyme of our times that sets us on our way - to peace, to joy,

freefernity[1] forever - and it is the mending of our ways,

and the agreement of our days, not waste away our days –

Soar then

As on eagle's wings

And brings me to this point: That all should

know by now, and are bound to - bound and secured

for your inspection of this, with hope [so] that you all might receive,

that which you are prepared to garner

for the nourishment of the spirit [in you all],

which happily awaits your reception of this feast. And it is for each of you

[that] this reception has been planned - so augured to permit you to come,

apprising you of these feats, and expectantly awaiting

your timely arrival, at this panacea of life.

CANTO I.

[for] There are many things to be considered in
life – the interpolation of sea and mist, rotations of heavenly
spheres, relative movements of these through time and space, whether to fly,
let spirit soar. The silver chord is the thread of truth we follow, and from the dust
of ages past, gone long ago, there comes alive again that which we with each
moment rediscover: A wealth of understanding that presages the coming of a world that is
life, liberty and a happiness which transcends all that we've known 'til now. Yet in its
wake, inexorable change. Mighty, noble, magnificence such as has not been
witnessed, Oh! these twelve thousands of years – the building,
the razing of ranges of mountains, or the forging of streams long and bending -
a sampling of grand moments these - huge, leviathan, majestic -
the work is sudden, complete. All's well that ends, [and] so begins anew.
Generals, statesmen, empire builders, and folly such as these, strut their stuff 'cross a
mighty, ignoble span – bridging chasms, sophic voids wide and deep.
Yet one which brings at long last the truth of all ages.
Now there have been men, truly great men, who have toiled this earth with love
and devotion, so that true knowledge and true wisdom should not perish –
and it is said that truth never dies.
Here then, is a truth: That all humanity should have borne across
the aeons of time, that promise of many a splendorous thing – To soar heavenwards –
To see the light and life which radiates from all that is –
To turn one's ear, to witness that spirit of life which is: Ah!
The mighty hum the planets make – Jupiter, Saturn, Uranus, Neptune,
Mercury and Pluto, Venus and Mars –
The Sun and the Moon – the tones they make, the vibrations they sew across the
fastnesses of inner space – The interlocking melodies they weave, and the impressions
they leave on us all. For we see only what our eyes tell us they see,
or hear what our ears hear, or what we taste, or touch, or smell. Here though,
where sound and color are one: A cosmic primer – the template for
Music, and Language, and Numbers,
reveals itself as the source, and substance of all that we know –
(lest inner seeing the Headwaters of our Universe)

CANTO II.

Cloy me soothes, and sweet were the days – Hyacinth, rosamundo –
lilac and odiferon[2]; petal fast, and fragrants such as these –
Golden glades and hues of every sigh and color – A hart bursts forth the
metamorphosis of spring – fishes race in stream and brook -
trout spotted, speckled and dragonfly. There are frogs, bullfrogs
and toads, there are periwinkles – Sparkling dew drops on leaf and limb.
Furthermore, this orchestral deluge of sight and sound
knows neither beginning, nor end.

CANTO III.

What is the difference between an animal and a
man; or for that matter, an angel?
Oh! Angels in the skies, light shining brightly – ever seeing, and time is
as nothing. Ward of sky and earth – yet no body has he.
Tyger brightly burning – what fierce, what grace! Power and beauty are mingled in
him. Has he, or any of his kind or any others though, a soul?
A spirit self? A tree, stationary as he is, has this,
And long life, and many years.
And man, what has he? In reality, as was intended, he has all these things.
He has body, he has spirit; and when both are one, as in days of old –
He has life, and light, and years.

CANTO IV.

'Cross moonbeams wide,
sea's waves glimmer, and
shimmer in the wind,
And far along a coastline hugged
a shore,
And I was there with you,
as before.
Midst interpolation of sea and mist –
Let spirit soar – to fly and be free
to see clear the way – this, is the congress, the great ingress of
life – and wonder of wonders –
It is the light, which is the life.

CANTO V.

We journeyed 'cross a wondering sea
Looked afar those days of old,
Nights brought stars and things,
Days were long. So we listened
deep within – midst the clamor,
the clangor of our world, and a voice
spoke within, neither heard, nor listened for;
Distance doesn't matter, time inconsequential…
It's the nearness, the closeness, deep within –
So come quiet, quietly come, so deep within -
the closeness, the nearness, the foreverness of now…
For as I've looked upon the World, and awakened
from a dream, the scenes they come alive –
What is it? We are the missing link.

There is pinkness, crimson, forests in the wind - birds fly -
and every moving, living thing upon the face of eternity -
The geographies of our mind's eye – inner seeing,
More beautiful than all of this that we see, hear, feel, taste, touch –
I smell a plot, and the words mean even less –
We can as easily spell reason like any other word that
Describes what we know, as far as it goes; and the twilight
Which lasts but a lifetime, is the world in which we live,
Casts a spell, forms a mold – verdigris, the decay which renders
Perceptions of a mind –'tis nonsense; and, so as not to confuse,
we'll spell that, like any other word; and the only way we know,
we'll spell it r-e-a-s-o-n, for it neither feels nor is aware of that which
goes beyond itself – But the World, this system of stars and bodies
are alive - Effortless vibrations, movements both large and small,
moving through time and space – What is it that we lack?

When I was a young man, space, infinity, life and death – all these things
were considered without prejudice – a dialogue unfettered by the dogma of a world
constrained unto itself by the lot of men – and a time soon came along –
We considered the exigencies of theory, notions, creeds and so on.
Well the contrariness of popular thinking became maddeningly burdensome for someone
Young as me, now don't pick and choose, don't even think – for as
limited as thinking may be, better to agree young man – accept the rhetoric
of an age – for it is confused – find a niche and forget – infinity, life, death,
and the great beyond – sleep, dream this life away, but I say, Now! Upon
the remembrance of things past, give this life meaning; for it sustains and succors
thanklessly, endlessly self-regulating – I, have wished to live as well.

What grace, what beauty dwells within each of us –
The plants, the trees and bubbling streams –
They do all that they do – ceaselessly – forever.
Endeavoring to emulate what is right and good,
I reach down – planted within me, tree of life,
Bubbling wellspring, there cascades forth the will
to be and to see, perceive rather more than
things simply as they appear to be, but as they are.

What is the answer to the riddle of life? What is the riddle?
What is it not? Is it not the seemingness of things?
Yes. It is that, and more, and less.
It is a puzzle that cannot be known.

Arguably a man of letters, whose world embraces all
knowledge is little more aware of his world as it is than
aboriginal man unburdened by the convolutions of his counterpart.
Is he (aboriginal man) any less rational in his will to survive,
to procreate, feed and foster his kind? Indeed – it is with clarity and cooperation,
and the understanding of earthly limitations, that provide him clues
as to the nature of life, with a relevance and clearness that defies the logic of his
more ideologically sophisticated counterpart.
Who has wondered at the marvels and complexities of life, and not
paused to consider the simple, well-ordered ways of the World –
There is truth in knowledge, and wisdom in truth. They should not be
confused, yet it is well and good to live, and better still to know how.

I've seen many things in Heaven and in the Earth, and not by much
did I hope for anything less than to impart directly to those who might wish to pause,
to reflect, not empty wonderings - to probe though, deeply beneath the
surface, those things long thought to be the intangible, subjective realities that
have but for a small few been little more than that - mere speculation.
A new day dawns – we transcend again the reckoning of an age,
Where new freedoms beckon - governed by immutable laws -
A Universe of possibilities, undreamed.

CANTO VI.

We flew heavenwards, until at last,

approaching a mighty forest, we descended,

lit upon the gentle banks of a vast shimmering pool;

where misted by the aerated spume of tumbling falls,

beheld a great crab[3] — Artemis perched

on its great glistening back,

And Effusion said to me:

"Homily, chanticleer - 'tis cornucopian[4], so nearly

Dear One - Grace this Page,

send us a line - A voice with

which we could rhyme -

Pegasean Mare, mere

moonlit night,

take these to hymn -

By Jove! Songs of Light -

Uranian Suite[5], fountain (head)

of Youth so clear -

Listen well friends (vortices)[6],

Joy to the Heart [and]

Great good cheer!"

MUSIC SCORES

URANIAN SUITE
in three movements

by John Lambert

II.

III.

CANTO VII.

I crossed a meadow by the moonlight
I saw the night, it grew out of sight
What's right, I love you.
And no one can see it, not even me.
Strong as the wind, we can't even see it.
Gentle, quiet as the breeze, I love you.
What's right, it grew out of sight
I saw the night, by moonlight
I crossed the meadow, I love you.
Strong as the wind - can't even see it.
Quiet as the breeze - I feel it
Bright as the moonlight - see it
Quiet as the breeze, strong as the wind -
We can't even see it
Gentle, quiet as the breeze, I love you.

CANTO VIII.

Let me see, if Heaven's needs satisfy me
I'm shaking, my heart is quaking
Let me see.
To think that we could understand
What needs, Heaven's be –
Wonderment, we can grow
But let me see, who runs the show
So we can know, which way to go
So the seed that we sow
Will last forever
In Heaven, and on Earth, below
Let me see if Heaven's needs satisfy me
I'm shaking, my heart is quaking
Let me see.

CANTO IX.

Why am I so high?
It came fast –
I saw it through looking glass mirrors,
And I wonder – why am I so high?
If you've tried dancing on waves
That thither and splash on rocks below,
It splashes me, and I dance on waves.
Like glass (fears – mind's troubles)
Weathers indifferently –
Harden, shatter – panes,
And you see me through them –
I have witnessed clarity,
Reasons that I know,
Celerity was done –
To quicken, fashion rapture –
Happiness is not look but don't touch.

CANTO X.

When we know there are three great things
And when we see, when we know
Times were for growing,

Look at this magnitude.
Largesse thee and bless me.
Now picture in your mind
Picture in your mind.

And greater than this
Look at four corners of life[7]
Where   there   is.
Abundantly flow the rivers of your life
And of all the ways
These proofs say we are,
Thank the lines
Spin the times
Spin the times.

CANTO XI.

Oh! Sing, sing of thee,

Living lessons of love.

Clouds rise on winding day.

Adventure smiles at the tufts of white and grey

Blue backdropped

At season's doorway to heavens

At season's doorway to heavens

And glad reply, and glad reply

Sing, oh sing of thee, in glad reply

Sing of the day

On beauty, caressed by nature

The performance witnessed we

To sing, sing, oh sing –

Tall trees

Their leaves are greening, and agreeing

Their leaves are greening, and agreeing

And when the fall comes

And when the fall comes

The seeing of our ways

The agreement of our days

Life speaks, and the winding dialogue ensues.

CANTO XII.

Titans struggle on planes of depth,

Wise men sending arts magical

Are a-treasured, all things measured.

We here linger, beyond comparisons unbounding

Lines of the vast spaces, of the last

Races of mankind.

Wherewithal, gladly approving to

Anyone, has these lines

They may know, as giants of wise men

Man is not without any of these things.

He knows, sings

He knows, sings

He knows, sings

Happy where there is a place

He can face himself, face to face

Glaring daringly upon arts magical

Wonderful, Wonderful

Beauty

CANTO XIII.

The islands of space grow small,
Machineries of thought
Catch light from afar,
Sources boundless, gather infinite
From light,
Grow, so we fight.[8]
I can tell you this friend,
If trappings be celeste,
You can gather me home.

CANTO XIV.

I went flying in the sky,
Double barrel sights the sites,
Never wonder why, we've been flying,
Saying simply this:
We've been trying to understand,
What we never knew before –
Oh! What's in store
For America,
Land of the free?
Some day we'll see, and remember
What we never knew before.
I've been flying,
Want to figure out a puzzle?
Pick a riddle,
Want to know why?
I rely on trying –
To want to know why,
To know why,
Know why,
Why –
I've been flying,
I've been flying –
Out to the World

Robin sits in its nest,
Crows are flying,
Men are dying, children are crying –
Won't you take a look around?
Do you see what I see,
Do you see what we've been?
And we call ourselves men,
These are our sins –
Oh! What could have been –
Some day we'll know,
And then we'll begin to grow,
Out to the World -
Where I've been flying,
Want to figure out a puzzle?
Pick a riddle,
Want to know why?
I rely on trying –
To want to know why,
To know why,
Know why,
Why -
I've been flying,
I've been flying -
Out to the World.

CANTO XV.

See the day, as it stands and glides past, on its way
Guess what things bring, the Songs of the Heart
And which is the part, not fleeing, but constance
This is what we: Chance of a Life
See the day, as it glides past, and stands to clearify
To know what things bring at last, Heart of the Songs
Part is the which, but constance, not fleeing
This is what we: Chance of a Life
See the Day as it stands, and glides past[9]

CANTO XVI.

Well, dreams are for living, seeing, believing
When not dreaming, but seeking, wanting to know
Hoping by groping and growing
Doing what seems right
False Pride's got you on a ride
Well dreams are for living, seeing, believing
When not dreaming, but seeking, wanting to know
Hoping by groping, and growing
Doing what seems right
False pride's got you on a ride -
Time to change it, rearrange it
Seasons come, go; and below, yeah
Green mountain meadows, birds sing in their nests.
We have yet time so little
Life's test has us in the middle, of Love –
Will see us through forever, together
And knowing that days of song, praise
Is the joy overflowing
In the knowledge of one's own inner beauty
The love that is Love

Seasons come, go; and below, yeah
Green mountain meadows, birds sing in their nests
We have yet time so little
Life's test has us in the middle of Love –
Will see us through forever, together
And knowing that days of song, praise
Is the joy overflowing
In the knowledge of one's own inner beauty
The love that is love
That is Love.

CANTO XVII.

Darkness comes, we await the light

Hearts are heavy, we'll not lose sight of the day

Frogs are croaking on the pond

That's where they belong, and beyond

So where were we when we've been wrong?

How many times is a lot

To remember what we are not?

To ransom a life away

To forget that we chose to be

And when we are not seeing, but singing

Feeling, dealing, reeling off the years

Is not what we thought it could be

And who would believe, all goes to the good?

Day break comes, we await the night

Hearts are rested, sun shines bright on the day

So they say, so they say

And we are believers in the Way of Ways

CANTO XVIII.

What we see, Oh! What we see is forever
So know that love is forever
Remember the days, how different they were
And seem to say, hey, this is what we see
How different it seems to be
To remind me of infinity
And love is forever
In it lies our strength, to live and to love
What we see, Oh! What we see is forever
So know that love is forever
Remember the days, how different they were
And seem to say, hey, this is what we see
How different it seems to be
To remind me of infinity
And love is forever
In it lies our strength, to live and to love
Our circle of life – To do right

CANTO XIX.

And when won was the day
And when done was the way
We were one so they say
This is life
This is what we are
This is life
We are knowing the truth
Of what we see, what we see,
And seeing:
Who we are, What we are, Why we are,
And why are we here?
Is it clear, why we're here –
We are forever, forever
If we would only remember, remember
We would be free, and then we'd see
Life's mystery –
So set about, re-route, turn around your life –
Find out what you must do
Go to the heart, and there you'll see
Heaven's mystery –
Know that we are changing,
Forevermore, forever, ever more

So sing a song of life
And our changing ways
Our changing ways, changing ways
Know that we are changing,
Forevermore, forever, ever more
Than we can know and sow that you sow
We can go to the heart
We can go to the heart
It's been that way, from the start
And now we know, now we know,
That what we see is the truth
The truth, the only truth
Love is forever, forever
Love is forever, forever
And so we'll see that to love is to be
And live eternally

So set about, re-route, turn around your life –
Find out what you must do
Go to the heart, and there you'll see
Heaven's mystery –
Know that we are changing,
Forevermore, forever, ever more
Than we can know and sow that you sow
We can go to the heart
We can go to the heart
It's been that way, from the start
And now we know, now we know,
That what we see is the truth
The truth, the only truth
Love is forever, forever
Love is forever, forever
And so we'll see that to love is to be
And live eternally

CANTO XX.

Here I stand, look all around me
In my paradise
Step into this world
Colors surround me
You should have seen, Oh! Ecstasy
Clearly reflects the changing dawn
Of the time that used to be
Seen from afar, I dance to melodies
Wandering among the times of time –
Sing a song, it's the only way to fly
Sing a song of pleasant memories
The skin of time touches me
Oh! Body beautiful
See Oh! Wondrous
Hear Oh! Wondrous
Pure and simple
Here I stand
Here I stand

CANTO XXI.

There is a queer thing
Here, in America.
Look at the World -
When you look at the World,
What do you see?
Linear Obsession.
Then, Tri-Linear Obsession is,
No doubt, one of…but…
How, and why, there are no
Discrepancies with…
There is a queer thing
Here, in America.

Look at the past,
Forward looking at the last -
Take the Eye of the Dollar,
Balance is the Key
Where our Thirteens[10], us to know,
We are about, in Atlantae –

That, is an obsession –
Many there are,
But three, in the main:
The first[11] -   (Be thee topmost):
A quick grab of the fact
Packed in, secondly: A wild stew canister
To the last,
A chew for your minding that also
Looking at
Thirdly:
Survival – Living the free life,
Learning, loving there

Upon thy threed obsession[12]

We are, dear fellows –

So, Be - Here – Now[13].

Take, nay, seek

The Way of Ways.

For it is in the first

We find the best –

From out of the past

We find at last –

Behold, Man's inherent Godhead[14]

That is:

My Father in Heaven

The Son, my me, and –

The Spirit, that is with us always.

So know this: Perform as one –

In Heaven

And

In the Earth

Then so obsess thee,

Then, and bless thee,

Then so on a three legged table

Rests a World:

Man:

I greet thee

The Universe

- Is Ours -

So take then also,

Look at America

Like this - eyes only –

A sham to think –

Take it with a prick,

The media cannot sting them;

But, ah me –

Look to my One: The Dollar is in the Balance

The Key is in the Eye

CANTO XXII.

Love's reason, for break or bond

And done, Oh! Break of day, comes the dawn

For sake of might

Lo, far from these unfettered isles,

And come by night, with thy desire

Unfleeting glimpse, unloose these bonds

With break of day, comes the dawn

So for love's reason

And far thee cry

While wait we for a season

Oh! By and by

The time for which we've been shown

Far from thee, when daily sown

Crown[15] venture, per adventure

Inclines me, binds me

Oh! These fettered isles

While watch we look to thee

Neither East Not West, nor plane of day

Yet with me be ever still

In my heart, where love's way.

The fire and the deep

We see by light

What we would have

And we would keep

Take care my love, and say no more
But watch my love, for what's in store
Neither reason, nor break nor bond
We embrace the glorious dawn
Unfettered isles, and soothing calm
So for all time – Love's reason,
Neither break, nor bond, magician's wand
And done, Oh! Break of day, comes the dawn

For sake of might
Lo, far from these unfettered isles
And come by night with thy desire
Unfleeting glimpse, unloose these bonds
With break of day, comes the dawn

CANTO XXIII.

What needs have we, that test time's plan
To know by number, the grains of sand
Invoke the oracle if you wish
But I will be true to thee, and in this
I sing and give love for all
Sing the song of life, the song of love
And speak the truth
For when I tell you
In love, all things great and small
Are for you and I, one and all

Consult the oracle, then, if you will
But I'll be true to thee ever still
Sing the song of life
And I'll be true to thee ever still
And sing the song of life
And tell you now, as for all time
Poet's verse, and couplets rhyme
Sing the song of life, the song of love
Sweet, sublime, true and pure
The sights, the sounds (eye and ear)
But know this –
Where reason pierces, transcends time and space
Is like the fish, who swims without the sea

So is my love, that would dry out

For want of reason's understanding

Comprehended not by mind

But swims within this sea of time

Where we sing of thee

Of love, beauty, wisdom, truth

And sings this vision's song

Of love and life, for now and all time

And I will be true to thee

Sing this song of love, and life

And you will see

That to be one, and be free

In love and life

Beauty, freedom, eternity

For in life's song, we sing this melody

And it is sweet, the song of life

That to love is to be, and live eternally

CANTO XXIV.

I saw it one night, as in a dream –
Radiance, beauty
Suffice, beyond these tenets of our mind
That binds, blinds, that winds and moved me
One night as in a dream –
Radiance, beauty
So, Oh! Dearly then – go to the wood
See thee light thy way
Strengthen this luminous body
Life's foods, energized water, and life-giving
One must see the Great Man

Text for Living
Pray often, approaching the altar
That is the Living Temple of Man
Kindred Spirits Unite in the Spirit of Love
And in making use of a vessel
He crosses the Great Water
Giving a form that receives unto itself
A perception of Life

Digression

A vessel that is a tool

Traverses the Great Waters.

The Temple of Man is a vessel, that filled

With the Creative, the energy of Life that we call Love

The energy of the Universe

That is God, means: God is Love,

The energy of Life, and all that is

And we, are one with Him

This is the Superior Man

He is again in the Absolute

Image and likeness of God, his maker

And on the Return from a fall from Grace

To the Garden of Eden, the Promised Land

To be in the presence of the Living, Loving God

And your Lord

And your Father in Heaven

This is the Great Man of the Text for the Living –

God, that is Love, and it is this, that I show you

I show you what is the Western Mountain[16]

Text for Living

Strengthen this Luminous Body

Life's foods, energized water and Life-Giving

One must see the Great Man

Text for Living

To do so, one must Pray often, approaching

The Altar that is the Living Temple of Man –

Kindred Spirits Unite in the Spirit of Love

And in a Universe of Dreams, there living in the

Presence, the Realm of God

Substance is the Land, Form lies without –

Your Father is the Great Man,

And again –

Text for Living

Making use of a vessel

He crosses the Great Water

Giving a form that receives

Unto itself a perception of life

Digression

A vessel that is a tool

Traverses the Great Waters.

The temple of Man is a vessel,

That filled with the Creative, the energy of life

That we call Love, the energy of life,

And all that is – And we are one with it.

This then is the Superior Man –

He is again in the absolute image and likeness of God,

For he has made of himself a vessel –

The energy is in him, thus he is moved to be one with it;

And his spirit makes the Great Crossing,

To be with the Father in Heaven where there is Love –

Where there is Love, there is God

And the Return from the Fall from Grace

To the Garden of Eden,

The Promised Land – To be with God

In the presence of your Living, Loving, Lord –

Your Father in Heaven,

Is to be with the Great Man, of the:

Text for Living

Forever, and ever

So shall it be defined:

The vessel, man, being thus, is able –

He traverses the Great Waters for all eternity –

He must see the Great Man –

Perseverance furthers, for then we shall

Meet face to face

Text for Living

The Life of the Father, it is this:

I show you what is the Western Mountain

Text for Living

Strengthen the luminous body

Filling it with the Creative Force

Crossing the Great Water –

One must see the Great Man

Be not afraid – there is success in what is fitting,

Do what is Right

Text for Living

To cross the Great Waters

One must make use of an unloaded boat,

Perseverance furthers. Sublime success.

One must, then see, the Great Man – and he will make of you

Fishers of Men

Text for Living

I will make you fishers of men

Fishers of men, fishers of men

I will make you fishers of men

If you follow me

Not just fishers of other men, but Fishers, themselves

Making use of unloaded boats

Casting to the Other Side

And all these things shall you do, as I have done

And more, so says the Great Man of the Text for Living,

if you follow (after) me.[17]

CANTO XXV.

You can be a goddess, if you know what I mean –
Soar as on eagles' wings and beyond –
The Dove means peace – Heaven in the Earth,
Neptune in Scorpio, Philosophy and Science.
The mind is the Door through which passes all understanding –
Knowledge of Life Eternal.
You, can be a Goddess, if you know what I mean.

The mind asserts, rather, rather this: it is through
The mind the assertion is made clear – Hypnotic induction
Achieves, as Don Juan puts it, a stopping of the World
Which surrounds us – I sing the Body Electric, Whitman said,
And, vivified while in this condition of receptivity
Which establishes the body of Humankind once and for All,
As the living vessel of the immaculate conception that is
Heaven in the Earth – it is through this that man shall know God.
So know dear one – this is what I mean when I say:
You, can be a goddess, if you know what I mean.

Be not the Snake

Nor the Scorpion stinging

Yet soar as on Eagles' wings –

And beyond, the Dove means Peace – peace of Mind,

Heaven in the Earth, God in Man –

And the Eyes have it –

The Eye and the Mind's Eye[18]-

For it is by quieting the mind that man shall see again,

And know God.

Listen though then to the murmurings of the Heart, that never

Satisfied with anything less than to know, to feel God's love –

'Til then its needs remain as always, incessant, ever changing

The emptyings and fillings of the Loving Heart –

By God! Its works bring Joy!

You can be a Goddess, if you know what I mean.

CANTO XXVI.

Head-Hearty, lamb-lion down with a horn, Arthur Sinclair Pendragon,
A lamb with a horn added to its head, mounts upon the Wings of a Unicorn.

As for Herbals, it's what you put in them that counts.
Vital, energizing potents portend good lasting things as they last.
Counts it's what, that you put vortexial herbals cornucopian,
With a horn back, that makes it so.
Now a horn book – the horn book Sir Francis mentions in Love's Labour's Lost,
that horn book as he says teaches young boys letters.
A, b, backwards is ba. Ba with a horn added to his head is bacornucopian.
Capricornicopiously, the goat shares not of the power and light of the Lamb of God
to which he is entitled; while the Unicorn,
That here-to-fore mythical creature of song and legend is but a winged
Horse or mare, symbol of the earth, with a horn added to his head,
Guided by a man who has trod Saturn's path.
He, is a Man with a horn added.

Bacornucopiously, this Man, this Unicornicopian shares
Of the power and light of the Lamb of God, to which he is now entitled,
For he has overcome his heart with his head, through quietus and prayer.
So that the ba, with the horn on his head is the lamb,
Aries, head lain down-a-lion with Leo's heart; in this way forming
The glyph for Capricorn, and its inherent Saturnian limitations (possibilities).
So Satan, get thee behind me; this is no ordinary Horn Book;
This goat has a horn on its head.

As for Herbals, it's what you put in them that counts.
Vital energizing potents portend good lasting things as they last.
Counts it's what, that you put vortexial herbals cornucopiously
With a horn back that makes it so - for when the lion lies down with the lamb,
And the heart is quieted by the head, a horn is added to the bridge of the eyes.

A horn added to the bridge of the eyes, spanning the endorphin producing pituitary
gland facilitates the entry of enkephalinic peptides onto the floor of the
Third ventricle (a cranial bridge), which in turn makes possible the de-calcification
Of the pineal gland, with its latent photoscopic cells; and it is in this way that the
Philosopher's Stone is finally realized for what it is, and rolled aside -
For a horn added to the bridge of the eyes receives into itself the creative force that is God,
and out of the darkness comes a light.
The light of the body is the eye. If therefore thine eye be single,
The whole body shall be full of light –
and the Unicorn, a winged mare with a horn added,
symbol of the earth, guided by a Man that has
Overcome his heart with his head through quietus and prayer,
Soars Heavenwards on Wings of Glory.

CANTO XXVII.

Oh! There is a way that men might see God -
the speed, the velocity with which the Heavens roar -
Sweet melodies that will surely show
that which we may someday know.
Step up, for arising to this occasion,
We shall build a firm foundation -
A fine blend, to pray, to allay your fears, this
you must do: There's power in the mountain, there's energy too -
coursing through this land of ours, pools of it -
In the darkness you will see, pass through dreaming sleep -
Find a mountain, where streams converge, again, there is
within a pyramid deep, in grottos sound asleep -
Rest, dream no more, but live, and giving gifts anew,
and I will show you a thing [or two].
Take these pieces, they're a puzzle that might be known,
I've shown it you before, Oh! 'Twas long, long ago;
Yet today's the day, for the play's had it in ways daily shown,
Yet we've known, a seed was planted, then grown to be –
Look far away, where there's peace enough; though within,
a practice of truth you must begin –
Find a path, take a willow switch -
Find another, and another, and where these paths converge,
There, there upon that point walls you must make,
The height by one point five seven, that's a base,
And each side at fifty one degrees, five minutes you will lay,
The sides, one point four nine by the height again they are;
Then two thirds up within you must lie, builded of granite,
with crystals of quartz, imbued a cap that's sheets of gold,
for there in a trance so deep, the treasure that you seek,
will set you free – pass through dreams and darkness you will see.
Reach out, focus lines that you may fill, 'tween eyes, with sounds
And color swirling 'round; pulse down, now up, and down again –

This fine hum that you have made, it's said, the spirit sings with

Life anew, and it's this I've longed to show; that the spirit within

you all, springing forth, and flying to heaven's deep –

And this you will surely see, all that is, and life's mysteries –

For again – the streams, radiant streams, 'neath crust and earth,

for ages – times from days of old, and mountains seated there mute,

Yet deep within – Atomics these, a fusion terrestrial, celestial

It is, then not at all, 'tis something else again, which when put to use,

You must feed on this, it's a gift of life, that's what it is,

for it is life – and a trance deep, self-hypnotized, 'neath dreams

You will be self-realized; for the Spirit reaching out and taking hold –

Canto XL[19] has it, and the Gita, treatise sixty six[20]; and

Mathew, chapter six, verse twenty-two[21]; and the dollar has, the

Great Seal, the Order of a New Way, which will reveal: Annuit Coeptis,

Novus Ordo Seclorum[22], with which you, my brethren can be free, and be

clear – for He blesses our beginnings –

Consider then, so simply put – that in many times, and in so many ways,

The truth, it is the same (has, and always will be)

For if you can decipher, cast aside, poetic license you will find here -

midst all these things resides – truths, my friends,

That have always been – For in heaven, there is contained

the secrets, which have remained, an inner chord, that's always been,

kept silent 'til one day our spirit soared to heights beyond the ken of men –

Where peace and light and love and more, to heights unknown our

Spirit soared – brought forth one day, that which has been restored -

the silence that has always been and more, for the secret of life has been restored.

And so all might know that which makes your spirit soar –

Pass then brethren, through this door,

For by a sacred, silver cord, to peace, to light

And love, life's reward:

The Order of a New Way, for now, and for always.

CANTO XXVIII.

Moods shift
And clouds lift
And splaying corners[23] tell –
Come to the well, friend,
By and by – Come to the Well
Streams course through the land
Streams, and sweet seeming
beams lights glorious
that teems, and lights that
lore in us –
There's a part of a man
At the heart of the plan,
Listen, listen –
Handily done, the weaver
has spun, arts cunning,
Arts magical, wondiferously
sew – you seem to be,
leave us, retrieve us at last,
reprieve us our past [up] days long ago.
A changing there has been,
A rearranging now and then –
Reprioritize at first the days
And then our ways,
So that fruit blossoms forth,
leaves limb, trunk and root,
So absolute is the telling of our tale –
Come to the well, friend
By and bye – Come to the Well.

Now some have known
And tried to've shown, a way.
Some by song and note
Some by plays they wrote –
All by word and deed,
True men loved and labored ceaselessly.

There is a fountain clear
Running, running
in the mountain deep,
in grottos sound asleep,
Awakened now, the summit reached
Mountains of men
Plumbed deep within
Pinnacle of desire
Rising higher and higher
[where]
Moods shift
And clouds lift
And splaying corners tell –
Come to the well, friend,
By and by – Come to the well.
Streams course through the land
Streams, and sweet seeming
Beams, lights glorious,
That teems, and lights that
Lore in us,
There's a part of a man
At the heart of the plan,
Listen, listen –

Handily done, the weaver has spun
Arts cunning, arts magical
Wondiferously so – you seem to
Believe us our past [up] days long ago –
A changing there has been,
A re-arranging now and then –
Reprioritize at first the days
And then our ways,
So that fruit blossoms forth,
Leaves, limb, trunk and root,
So absolute is the telling of our tale -
Come to the well, friend -
By and bye - Come to the Well.

CANTO XXIX.

Cross Fields of Light[24],
Chargers[25] mounted,
Nights of the Round Table[26],
Twelve Days[27] of Christmas counted –

The Magis Tree
Merlin, raptor, presents
there: One: [a] game,
To: pray,
Then lit, from that tree
Soared: Excalibur
In stone it says removed by Art
makes Three: Wise men

Twelve Days of Christmas counted,
Nights of the Round Table,
Chargers mounted –
Cross Fields of Light,
Crowns blazing there,
Pearl of Great Price,
Gift so rare:
For lo! This lofty Instauratio
Bright,
Man's one present[:] Hope -
The Magistry of Christmas
is God's Delight!

CANTO XXX.

Beyond the reach of time,
Heaven's Galactic Keep,
where nights' eternal band
and rainbows brightly sweep -

There's singing far from you and me
and wonder midst a timeless sea;
Eternal swale, a telling tale,
That's long, and bright, and deep.

Beauty's dusk, dreams lie waking –
higher than we lore,
Travelers moving out from here
to some far, some glorious shore.

For time we know, is but a glimpse,
a place we've been before
which comes home shining now to me –
angelic choir, celestial sea
and Time's timelessness abound;
For life and love are but these
three: Light, and Color and Sound.

So to our earthly mount,
To pray, alight the Way –
and glory is a place for some
who know but peace on earth –
But if Heaven be God's Ah! Men,
Then Man is God's Rebirth!

Out beyond the reach of Time,
Heaven's Galactic Keep,
where nights' eternal band,
and rainbows brightly sweep –
There's singing far from you and me
And wonder midst a timeless sea;
Eternal swale, a telling tale,
That's long and bright, and deep.
Beauty's dusk, dreams lie waking
higher than we lore,
Travelers moving out from here
To some far, some glorious shore.

CANTO XXXI.

You know I'm just a traveler,
a wanderer on his way,
I've journeyed far, and lo these years,
I mean aeons long gone, and yet to be –
What is the truth we seek?
It is, our inward guide –
Though stars and space lie outward bound –
'tis love that shows us why.
So look to those outer stars, and deep within,
where we touch, and our light shines and shows for now
and all time the way of peace –
For I am a man, who lives on the edge of a world
sowing and reaping, giving and gaining, the fruit of the living.
Oh! Wanderer, pathfinder among the stars –
You've ceased to wonder, and found your place in time
Non-existential – It's where you are
That you've looked 'cross vast and mighty plains,

The deeps you've plumbed within your soul,
And so I say: Be no more afraid
Shed not even a tear,
For I am with you always.
Though storm clouds rain, snows fall,
and icy roads bar your way – I am
with you always. Look not without
For love, for it is all around.
Fear neither man nor beast, tread paths high and good, alone,
or in the company of your brethren, friends, lovers
of my soul, and know, remember,
Traveler – you've come Oh! so far,
And the way lies long and hard –

Yet that truth which you seek, and
the key to life's eternal mystery,
and time's unending illusion lies within
You all – for I am with you always.

So traveler – live, and dream
and work this truth in all that you may do,
for as you live, I live also -
As you dream, I dream; and together,
on the edge of the World, we shall work many miracles,
until one day – we, shall illumine the four, far corners of the earth
For the way of peace, for all men, and all time –
travelers, lovers of my soul, lies within –
For I am with all of you always, forever –
Even until the ends of the earth.

Oh! Light that shines so brightly,
in the Heavens deep -
It is the way, it is, the way –
So travel far, travel far and wide –
for it is the God in you that shines so bright,
It's the God in you that makes this light –
To illumine the four corners of our home, this is our earthly deed –
To work, and love, and give of ourselves, these are our earthly seeds –
For we are men, planted so dearly here, with care and wise good patience,
So that we might persevere –
For there is hope my friends in what is good,
and grace in all we do;
Where deep within, we give our light and life,
Our love springs forth anew –
'Til peace come, and godspeed, to our earthly home,
where lines were writ, and tomes were made,
Messages to the living: it's love and light
and nothing more, that is worthy of our giving –

So go now, grow now –
Strong, and straight, and true
'Cause what you've done, you've shown a way,
You've said your piece, you've had your say –
Come now then, oh so dearly –
where earth's life streams cross,
and the stars see thee light thy way –
for under a pyramid, a man-god, a knower of the truth;
neither journeys, nor travels, nor wanders ever again;
for he is, he knows, that I am the Way,
the truth, and the light of the living;
and I shall be with you always,
even, unto the ends of the earth.

CANTO XXXII.

Roll aside the Philosopher's Stone
For in a secret place, there is, left alone,
a singular entryway, where Hope lies waiting.
A Hope that lights a way,
a conscious reverie, a remedy:
Nameless, a voice that speaks of a stone rolled away,
And entreats, alone, of a day that changed forever
One man's life on earth – for there,
'Twas in a flash: Entertainment borne on the
Life strings of his soul.

CANTO XXXIII

But for now, I sit alone,

a traveler resting weary feet – I slake

a parched throat, yet it is a mind's continuous thirsting after

refreshments cerebral which I seek, so catatonic I sit – Ephemeral

blessings, guessing at the truth have little place here – they

fend not on me – but the world loves a new and tonal blessing –

Fancies' changes blown by winds that exchange feast, for famine.

Examine this:

Where lies a road, beats marked on stones clearly sending,

unending it is – cyclical revisitations, marked by notches in the plan –

That is in the nick of time we see, preternatural pinings, opining us these things -

constitutionally forged – Turned in a furnace whose fire and heat,

these mettlesome tracts exact the constancy contained therein.

So molded, emboldened – Ah, Sweet mirth!!

The smith wields, and welds –

Not his alone – though wholly contrived –

Arrived upon-derous thing –

Delicately balancing the act, contractually –

Truly holding truest, to that which blinds: Light, heat –

Shapes and forms containing substantially all things in them which are -

Unchanging in this way – will ever be.

CANTO XXXIV

Ah! Rest me now –

Labors never ceasing –

Releasing once again that tenuous hold that we seek

- to be the harvest queen[28] -

- kingdoms of our world -

Hasten to the lasting, moments unseen, charted on the wings of

My soul ever seeking where, when rests at last

There's a place, my home I see.

Vivify, ensorcel me now, on this I pray -

Enchantress, entreating us these things:

Twin pillars, belike the gates of Knowledge,

where Castor and Pollux sit astride wisdom and truth -

Portals through which you must surely pass,

Making steadily your way,

foreign though these things be,

Relieved at last, that which is lasting,

Ends, in a way: That means:

So sit beside that long river, never ending,

While the craft, your soul, pilots ways past shoals unseen -

Master, guide and grant me this:

Voyager, pilgrim –

Enjoin your heart, your mind, your soul to be one with me,

and these scenes so seen to be, will be.

For…

CODA

We are the giants in the earth
We are the gods of our universe

Every blade of grass, the infinity in a
Moment - And the reasons are for love, and the
equanimity of space, the content of which we are afforded
the necessity of giving light to a wealth of understanding beyond
this quantum leap – for the denouement of life unfolds before our eyes,
we see the infinity of man and the consciousness of love,
the soul song, the energy of life itself.
It tells a tale of lightening up the
skies of our minds, loosens the burden of fear
with the knowledge of life eternal.
We are the giants in the earth.

The distinction in seeking after truth
is in the blueprint of the ages,
and seen but once, and go forever with you, so be it.

Then nourish like a seed the growth of
mind, body, and spirit [is the guiding light, and
a light it is] the spark which lives in the body proper - whose
initial awakening is tantamount to ecstasy nonpareil - that is indeed but
a spark, for it is only the beginning, as compared to
the fruition of which it signals the awakening of a giant in the earth.
As the mind seeks to acquaint itself with the
Inherent design of the body electric,
Dimensia is lost.
Minding the Body awakens the Spirit in man,
avers that this transformation is at hand, figuratively,
and so on and on, until these things are done, we'll
be separate and not one. But by one way, there is, truth.

Love is the energy of the universe.

In it lies our strength to live and to love - again and again - physically,

where this process takes form; mentally, where the decision

and direction to do so were given; wherein the Spirit, substance of all –

Awakened first by the spirit in man, then the body, mind, and back again,

sufficiently energized, achieves equanimity with its parts, and the body entire.

These three agents (body, mind and spirit), then acting as one,

move to become united with that part of life which is spirit - pure energy,

where-there-is-life eternal in spirit - and this is the truth of it:

One by one we will surely come to realize these things.

Some fine time this equanimity we speak of will be reached in ourselves,

and finally, all potential resolved - in the universe as well.

Another cycle will be complete, things will be as they once were, and I can

see it now: Albert's Einstein will read differently than this E=mc2 that we

are presently limited to, and the Pineal equation will read E=E.

So the neophytes will wonder at this, let their minds seek to probe as I have

for the answer that cannot be found [by intellect alone]. So I do this, and here it is:

We are the giants in the earth

We are the gods of our universe

Almighty father in Heaven, thanks be these praises fixed to shine - and it is

the line and rhyme of our times that sets us on our way - to peace, to joy,

freefernity[29] forever - and it is the mending of our ways,

and the agreement of our days, not waste away our days –

Soar then

As on eagle's wings

And brings me to this point: That all should

know by now, and are bound to - bound and secured

for your inspection of this, with hope [so] that you all might receive,

that which you are prepared to garner

for the nourishment of the spirit [in you all],

which happily awaits your reception of this feast. And it is for each of you

[that] this reception has been planned - so augured to permit you to come,

apprising you of these feats, and expectantly awaiting

your timely arrival, at this panacea of life.

END NOTES

1   *Freefernity. Freedom in eternity, life without beginning or end*

2   *The sweetest smelling flower we can know*

3   *The Great Crab references the moon. The eight legs stand for the phases of the moon. The most likely time that a human can synchronize with lunar harmonics is about 9 days before a full moon to 3 days after. Celestial plus terrestrial energies come together – the strongest time for prayer. Fusion – Using man as a vessel for the life force, mana*

4   *The cornucopia, the Horn of Plenty, in the shape of a vortex (chakras), as is the unicorn horn. The chakras are how we interact with Energy. See Chakras, C.W. Leadbeater; and the I Ching, Hexagram 2, Wilhelm-Baynes translation 1967*

5   *Uranian Suite. Also, in the <u>I Ching</u>, Hexagram 11, Bringing heaven down to earth.*

6   *Vortices, the chakras*

7   *Four corners of life. The four elements, earth, air, fire and water*

8   *Fight. To strive, endure, persevere*

9   *This palindrome consists of two parts. The first part provides the questions; the second, answers.*

10 *Thirteen colonies of America*

11 *And that which Bucke refers to as 'cosmic consciousness', Richard Maurice Bucke M.D., Cosmic Consciousness*

12 *Which, as stated consists of these three main points: 1. Physical contact with God; 2. Expression of this as truth; and 3. The survival necessary for the realization of all of the above*

13 *That is to say: engage in one area of life at a time, and in each of these, do so to the best of your ability, always*

14 *A tri-linear fact in and of itself, whereby a man is made whole. For when his conscious self and low-self or spirit comes face to face in the dwelling place of the most high with the father or high-self, and these three physical aspects of his nature begin for the first time to function as a fully integrated whole, then, it can be said without qualification that he is at long last and for all time truly something which has been created, form and substance in the image and likeness of God; and it is this realization that is his salvation. It will set him free*

15 *Crown refers to the seventh chakra.*

16 *The Western Mountain –1967 – a great pyramid. See I Ching, Hexagram 26, Wilhelm-Baynes translation 1967*

17 *See Book of Matthew, <u>Holy Bible</u>, King James Version of 1611*

18 *Pituitary and Pineal*

19 *Canto XL enumerates differences and chakratic function according to the principles laid down by C.W. Leadbeater in Chakras*

20 *The Baghavad Gita, Chapter 18, Text 66*

21 *Book of Matthew 6:22, Holy Bible, King James Version of 1611, "The light of the body is the eye: If therefore thine eye be single, thy whole body shall be full of light."*

22 *"Annuit Coeptis" – He blesses our beginnings. "Novus Ordo Seclorum" – Order of a New Way*
    According to Richard S. Patterson and Richardson Dougall, Annuit cœptis (meaning "favours our undertakings") and the other motto on the reverse of the Great Seal, Novus ordo seclorum (meaning "new order of the ages"), can both be traced to lines by the Roman poet Virgil.

23 *Splaying corners – the apex [of a pyramid]*

24 *The View Over Atlantis, Mitchell*

25 *Love's Labour's Lost, 5-1, Shakespeare (Bacon), "Do you not educate youth at the charge-house on the top of the mountain?"*

26 *Stonehenge, Salisbury, England*

27 *Hyper-Number Theory, Dr. Charles Muses, Consciousness and Reality*

28 *Ceres, goddess of fruits*

29 *Freefernity. Freedom in eternity, life without beginning or end*